NATURAL, ARTIFICIAL & MAN-MADE

JEN BREACH

Rourke™

Before Reading: *Building Background Knowledge and Vocabulary*

Building background knowledge can help children process new information and build upon what they already know. Before reading a book, it is important to tap into what children already know about the topic. This will help them develop their vocabulary and increase their reading comprehension.

Questions and Activities to Build Background Knowledge:

1. Look at the front cover of the book and read the title. What do you think this book will be about?
2. What do you already know about this topic?
3. Take a book walk and skim the pages. Look at the table of contents, photographs, captions, and bold words. Did these text features give you any information or predictions about what you will read in this book?

Vocabulary: *Vocabulary Is Key to Reading Comprehension*

Use the following directions to prompt a conversation about each word:

- Read the vocabulary words.
- What comes to mind when you see each word?
- What do you think each word means?

Vocabulary Words:
- artificial
- domestication
- foraged
- ingredient
- manipulated
- pollinated

During Reading: *Reading for Meaning and Understanding*

To achieve deep comprehension of a book, children are encouraged to use close reading strategies. During reading, it is important to have children stop and make connections. These connections result in deeper analysis and understanding of a book.

 Close Reading a Text

During reading, have children stop and talk about the following:

- Any confusing parts
- Any unknown words
- Text-to-text, text-to-self, text-to-world connections
- The main idea in each chapter or heading

Encourage children to use context clues to determine the meaning of any unknown words. These strategies will help children learn to analyze the text more thoroughly as they read.

When you are finished reading this book, turn to the next-to-last page for **After-Reading Questions** and an **Activity**.

TABLE OF CONTENTS

VANILLA:
THE FLAVOR DIVA

Vanilla gives cookies and cakes their deliciously wonderful flavor. Surprisingly though, only about one percent of vanilla used in cooking and vanilla-scented items, like candles, is natural. The rest, about 99 percent, is man-made. This is because natural vanilla is hard to farm.

Natural vanilla comes from vanilla orchids, which only grow in a few places throughout the world. The flower on the orchid needs to be **pollinated** to develop seed pods of vanilla flavor. But the orchid only flowers one day a year, and vanilla orchid pollinators are rare. Because of this, vanilla must be pollinated by hand.

pollinated (POL-uh-neyt-ed): to be fertilized

It's not surprising, then, that vanilla was the first **artificial** flavor ever developed. By 1875, scientists had mapped the vanilla flavor compound and could make the same compound artificially from processed pine bark. This method is still used now to make artificial vanilla.

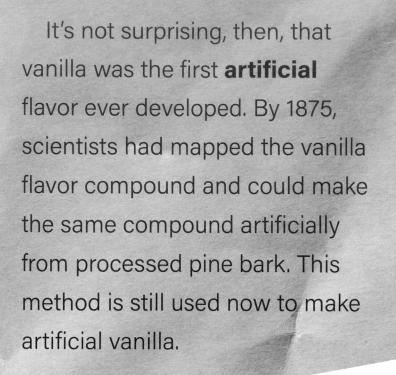

BEAVER BUTTS

For a time, artificial vanilla was harvested from beavers. Beavers have a vanilla-scented musk that they use to mark their territories. The scent is vanilla-y because the beavers eat pine bark!

artificial (ahr-tuh-FISH-uhl): produced by humans rather than by nature

CUMIN: THE GLOBAL SPICE

Cumin is native to the Middle East, and its warm, earthy flavor comes from its seeds. It is listed as an **ingredient** in the world's oldest recipe, which was written in Iraq in 1750 BC. At that time, the Middle East was the source of much of the world's trade, including wheat, gems, paint pigments, and spices. Cumin found a spot on those trade routes to ancient Greece and Rome, Middle Ages Europe, Africa, India, and China. Cumin made its way to South America with the Spanish invasion in the 1500s. It became an important flavor in all these regions' cuisines.

ingredient (in-GREE-dee-uhnt): one part of a mixture

CUMIN'S CULTURAL IMPORTANCE

Historically, couples in Europe would carry pouches of cumin at their wedding for good luck. In medieval Germany, cumin seeds were baked into bread to prevent wood-elves from stealing the loaves. Ancient Egyptians used cumin in the preparation of mummies!

One reason that cumin was such a popular spice was that the plant was very easy to grow. People could access it easily and cheaply.

SAFFRON: THE MOST EXPENSIVE FOOD

Saffron, which turns food a vibrant yellow color in cooking, tastes a little floral and a little sweet. It is an important ingredient in Spanish paella, French bouillabaisse, Kashmiri curry, and Indian biryani. By weight, it is the most expensive food on the planet.

FAKE SAFFRON IS BIG BUSINESS

No one has been able to create artificial saffron, so selling fake saffron to trick consumers is big business! Yellow turmeric, a cheaper spice, has been labeled and sold as "ground saffron." Red silk fibers and dyed horsehair have been sold as "saffron threads."

Saffron is harvested from small purple flowers that bloom once a year in Iran. Each flower produces three delicate red threads of saffron that must be picked by hand. It takes seventy thousand flowers to produce one pound of saffron! This method of harvesting saffron has stayed the same for thousands of years.

CORN: AN AMERICAN CROP

Thousands of years ago across modern-day Mexico, corn grew as a wild grass and was **foraged** by American Indians. Eventually, they planted corn on purpose and tended the crops. For the past 1,000 years, corn has been common across both North America and South America.

foraged (FOR–ijd): collected as wild food

Wild corn had small, tough kernels. American Indians selectively cultivated the corn to produce better corn. They saved and replanted the seeds from plants that had more kernels on bigger cobs to develop the delicious corn we eat today.

Corn is very important to the United States—it is the most common crop farmed, and corn products are included in hundreds of foods, such as cornmeal, cornstarch, corn oil, and corn syrup.

DOMESTICATED FOODS: CHICKENS, CARROTS, AND MORE

Many common foods in American kitchens cannot be found in the wild. They are the result of **domestication**.

There are more chickens than any other bird on the planet, but chickens only exist because of human intervention. They are a species of red jungle fowl, a wild tropical bird found in India and southeast Asia. Humans began domesticating red jungle fowl around 8,000 years ago. They selectively bred birds that grew quickly and laid a lot of eggs. What they created are chickens that can grow three times faster than red jungle fowl. These chickens provide more meat and eggs for farmers to sell.

domestication (duh–mes–ti–KAY–shuhn): the process of adapting wild plants or animals for human use

Wild carrots first grew in what is now modern Afghanistan. More than 5,000 years ago, carrots were only used for their tops and seeds. The root, which wasn't used, was small, hard, and pale yellow or white. Persian people began selectively farming carrots for the root, which is the part of the carrot that we eat now. They were yellow, white, purple, or orange. The orange variety grew best in the wet weather of the Netherlands, the biggest agricultural country at the time, and so it became the standard color for carrots.

WHAT ELSE IS DOMESTICATED?

Most of the fruits and vegetables in the supermarket are domesticated: oranges, lemons, bananas, grapes, strawberries, apples, pears, sweet potatoes, peppers, green beans, tomatoes, potatoes, apricots, peaches, mangoes, cucumbers, watermelons, and more.

GMOS: MAN-MADE FOODS

Humans have **manipulated** food for thousands of years through selective breeding, but in the last few decades we have been able to manipulate food in a laboratory to create genetically modified organisms (GMOs).

manipulated (muh-NIP-you-late-ed): changed or altered the state of something

By changing the DNA of a plant, food scientists can increase crop yield, speed up growth, make plants resistant to pests, make them more nutritious as feed for animals, and even give them a longer shelf life in the supermarket.

More than 90 percent of corn, beets, and soybeans currently grown in the United States are genetically modified. While GMOs can provide cheaper, bigger harvests, they are putting at risk the biodiversity of plants and the wild animals and insects who rely on those plants for food or habitat.

SAFE AND SOUND IN SVALBARD

In Svalbard, Norway, buried deep beneath an ice-covered mountain, is the Global Seed Vault. The Global Seed Vault is an archive of billions of dormant seeds from around the world, cataloguing and preserving plant genetic diversity. In the last 250 years, nearly 600 plant species have gone extinct. Forty percent of the world's current plant population is endangered. This rapid rate of extinction is due to human intervention, including climate change.

The location of the Global Seed Vault is key: its natural surrounding of permafrost keeps the seeds frozen so they can be used years from now if needed.

CUMIN-ROASTED CARROTS

— INGREDIENTS —

5   medium carrots, peeled
2   tablespoons extra virgin olive oil
    salt and freshly ground pepper (to taste)
½   teaspoon cumin
½   teaspoon coriander (optional)
2   tablespoons unsalted butter, at room
    temperature
½   teaspoon turmeric
½   teaspoon chili powder
2   tablespoons chopped fresh mint or any
    other herb (optional)

— INSTRUCTIONS —

1. Preheat the oven to 425°. Cut the carrots into thick coins. In a bowl, toss with oil, salt, and pepper.

2. Put the carrots in one layer on a sheet pan. Roast for 25-40 minutes, depending on how crunchy or soft you like them. Turn the carrots once while baking.

3. In a bowl, stir together the spices and butter.

4. When the carrots are ready, toss them in the bowl with the spiced butter and herbs, if using. Add salt and pepper to taste.

INDEX

AFTER-READING QUESTIONS

1. Natural vanilla comes from vanilla orchids. What are two ways to create artificial vanilla?

2. What is the difference between natural flavor and artificial flavor?

3. Name five domesticated foods available in the United States.

4. Where is the Global Seed Vault located?

5. Which three crops that are grown in the United States are almost entirely genetically modified?

ACTIVITY

Find three to five spices or flavors in your family's kitchen cupboards. Write down what each one tastes and smells like and where you think they come from. Now do some research and see if you are right!

ABOUT THE AUTHOR

Jen Breach (pronouns: they/them) is queer and nonbinary. Jen grew up in a tiny town in rural Australia with three older brothers, two parents, and one pet duck. Jen has worked as an archaeologist, a librarian, an editor, a florist, a barista, a bagel-baker, a code-breaker, a ticket-taker, and a trouble-maker. The best job they ever had was as a writer, which they do now in Philadelphia, Pennsylvania. Jen loves to cook and has a full spice rack that includes vanilla, cumin, and saffron.

www.rourkebooks.com

PHOTO CREDITS: Cover: Curioso.Photography/ Shutterstock.com; page 5: Kletr/Shutterstock.com; page 6: Krisana Antharith/Shutterstock.com; page 7: BMJ/Shutterstock.com; page 7: Aquarius Studio/Shutterstock.com; page 8: AAR Studio/Shutterstock.com; page 9: Lokman Shekh/Shutterstock.com; page 10: StockImageFactory.com/ Shutterstock.com; page 11: Narciso Arellano on Unsplash; page 11: Dineshahir/Shutterstock.com; pages 12-13: orinocoArt/Shutterstock.com; page 13: marco mayer/Shutterstock.com;
page 14: Gts/Shutterstock.com; pages 14-15: MORTEZA NIKOUBAZL/SIPA/Newscom; pages 16-17: Jen Theodore on Unsplash; page 16: Grafissimo/ Getty Images; page 18:vainillaychile/Shutterstock.com; page 18: Pheonix Han on Unsplash; page 19: Elena Schweitzer/Shutterstock.com; page 19: Viktoria Hodos/Shutterstock.com; page 21: Jamil Bin Mat Isa/Shutterstock.com; page 21: Moonborne/Shutterstock.com; page 21: badnews86dups/Shutterstock.com; page 22: Kennerth Kullman/Shutterstock.com; page 23: Bildagentur Zoonar GmbH/Shutterstock.com; page 24: TheLazyPineapple/Shutterstock.com; page 24: Djordje R/Shutterstock.com; page 24: Swapan Photography/Shutterstock.com; page 24: Hong Vo/Shutterstock.com; page 24: Fabio Boccuzzi/Shutterstock.com; page 24: Anita van den Broek/Shutterstock.com; page 26: vlalukinv/Shutterstock.com; pages 26-27: iStock / Getty Images Plus; pages 28-29: Borkowska Trippin/Shutterstock.com; page 30: Brent Hofacker/ Shutterstock.com; pages: 3-4, 6, 8, 10-12, 14, 16, 18-20, 22, 24-26, 28, 30-32: Nas photo/ Shutterstock.com; pages: 1, 5, 7, 9-10, 13, 17-18, 21, 23, 25, 30-32: Lana Veshta/ Shutterstock.com; pages: 6-7, 21: Ales Krivec on Unsplash

Edited by: Catherine Malaski
Cover and interior design by: Max Porter

Library of Congress PCN Data

Natural, Artificial, and Man-Made / Jen Breach
(Food Tour)
ISBN 978-1-73165-290-4 (hard cover)(alk. paper)
ISBN 978-1-73165-260-7 (soft cover)
ISBN 978-1-73165-320-8 (e-book)
ISBN 978-1-73165-350-5 (e-pub)
Library of Congress Control Number: 2021952200

Rourke Educational Media
Printed in the United States of America
01-2412211937